Walter Ronoghan

X X X X

CANAJAN, EH?

**OTHER BOOKS
BY
MARK M. ORKIN**

Speaking Canadian English
Speaking Canadian French
Legal Ethics
The Law of Costs

CANAJAN, EH?

MARK M. ORKIN

Illustrations by ISAAC BICKERSTAFF

General Publishing Company Limited Don Mills, Ontario

First published 1973 by
General Publishing Company Limited

Design: Brant Cowie

ISBN 0-7736-0022-1
Printed in Canada

Printed and bound in Canada by
T. H. Best Printing Company Limited, Don Mills, Ontario

**TO MY FATHER
AND MOTHER
WHO DISCOVERED
CANADA**

Let us get nearer to the fire, so that
we can see what we are saying.
                    The Bubis of Fernando Po

PREFACE

This book was made possible, not by a Canada Council grant but by my Grade Six teacher at Elgin Street Public School in Ottawa long ago.

On that far-off day the class was engaged in something called 'Memory Work', which turned out to be a serial recitation of Wordsworth's poem, 'The Solitary Reaper'.

The first reciter announced the title well enough, but stumbled badly on the opening line by placing the comma after the third word rather than before it, to produce:

> Behold her single, in the field
> Yon solitary Highland Lass!

When the teacher pointed out that the first line did not refer to the marital status of the Lass, this was well-received by the rest of the class, although so damaging to the reciter's self-possession that the rest of the stanza was inaudible.

Other memory workers followed with doubtful success until the final reciter, heedless of his predecessors' downfall, launched into the last verse with a confidence born of inexperience:

> Whate'er the theme, the maiden sang
> Ziff her song could have no ending;

only to be interrupted by the teacher who demanded to know in a voice of thunder (for teachers were much older, larger and fiercer in those days): 'What language is "ziff", boy? What language is "ziff"?' Whereupon the reciter, not knowing what to answer, fell silent as did the rest of the class, after a rustle of nervous laughter. The recitation was later resumed and soon finished, but the teacher's question remained in one pupil's mind, to quote the concluding words of the poem, 'Long after it was heard no more.'

In the many years which have passed since then, I have sometimes wondered what answer might have been made by the incomprehensible boy to the uncomprehending teacher. With this book I can offer a belated reply to that long unanswered question: ' "Ziff" is *Canajan*, Mr. Patterson.'

INTRODUCTION

Since it is a bilingual country Canada has four languages. This gives fullest scope to linguistic self-expression while considerably increasing the likelihood of misunderstanding.

It is customary to divide the Canajan population into *Francophone* and *Anglophone.** On the French Canajan side the fishle language is French, used for statutes, classics, scholarly journals and the things that nobody bothers to read. Most French Canajans, while they read and write French, talk Joual, the nash null language of Quebec. It is not necessary to teach Joual since every native son already speaks it. Besides, no manuals of instruction exist. Why should they?

On the English Canajan side the fishle language is English, the language of

---

**These terms are thought by some to derive from two early communications systems, one operated mainly in Quebec by la Mère Cloche and the other in English-speaking parts of the country by Ma Bell. As parallel groups of subscribers cohered around their respective party lines, the division of Canajans into two main linguistic communities developed into the social and political reality which we know today. The subsequent merger of the two telephone systems (whose head office was symbolically located in the Province of Quebec) occurred too late to materially affect the linguistic division of the country.*

parliamentary debates, Royal Commission reports, book reviews and all the speeches that no one bothers to listen to. Most English Canajans, although they are able to write English, talk Canajan, the nash null language of English Canada. As with Joual, no formal instruction in Canajan is either given or necessary. Who would need it? All Anglos speak Canajan from birth.

Some years ago a self-styled professor at the University of Sinney compiled a lexicon of Strine, the nash null language of Australia. I had hoped that his opposite number at the University of Tronna would accept the challenge and produce a study of Canajan, but this was to overestimate our academics' concern for Canajan content. Although the University of Tronna has long been known as a hotbed of Canajan (along with the University of Albirda at Kail Gree, and the University of Beesee) the language of instruction and research in these places has always been English. Canajan was and is consistently downgraded, ridiculed or ignored by our scholars.

In part this happened because Canajan academics have been far too busy suppressing (or supporting) demonstraders, and attacking (or defending) the nomination of Mare Cans to faculty appointments to devote much time to Canajan studies. They also feared that to call attention to the existence of Canajan might leave the impression that Anglos were illiterate – much as educated Quebeckers pretended until recently that Joual did not exist, while busily trying to wash it out of their children's mouths with soap and water. But fortunately such backward attitudes are passing away in both cultures, and with the growing Mare Canzation of our campuses we may look to see Canajan Studies (along with Joual Studies) accorded their rightful place in academic curricula. To help remedy this default the brief glossary of Canajan which follows has been compiled.

It may come as a surprise to many Anglophones to realize that they have been speaking Canajan all their lives. They may be even more surprised to discover that the main characteristics of Canajan are identical with those of Joual. For it is a fact that the two nash null languages of Canada display precisely the same qualities. These will emerge in the pages which follow, but for convenience they may briefly be listed as: a nimiety of neologisms, an impudicity of pronunciation, a crapulence of grammar, a prurience of syntax, and a necrosis of Mare Canisms.

No standard of Canajan has yet been established. Hence domestic readers may encounter some expressions here and there with which they are unfamiliar, but all specimens have been carefully gathered in the field. On the other hand, forners need exercise no caution in using this text since all terms discussed will be understandable by somebody somewhere in Canada. And all are, beyond question, Canajan.

A

AIR
To make mistakes. As in the Canajan proverb: 'To air is yoomin, toofer give duhvine.'

ALBIRDA
Province at the western end of the prayer ease, *q.v.* Noted for its natchurl resources, among them gassa noil. There is a school of Fie Narts at Bamf.

ALTSO	As well as; too. As in: 'They altso serve who oney stannan weight.'
ANGLO	A non-French Canajan Canajan.
AP ZURD	Ridiculous, preposterous. As in: 'It's jiss ap zurd, Linda, ta sear withim.'
ARDIC	The far north, home of the Esk Moze, one of Canada's two found-in races, *q.v.* Of or pertaining to northern areas, boreal.

The Ardic, as one of the world's leading producers of snow, benefitted for many years

ESKIMO CARVINGS

genuine
made in japan

from a high world demand for this commodity which reached its peak during the gold rush of '98. The market later became depressed during World War I, although it picked up again when the skiing craze swept Canada in the twendies and thirdies.

This boom proved short-lived, however, when the invention of artificial snow following World War II caused demand for the natural product to decline sharply. As a result the Ardic was left with vast stocks and no markets other than the Knighted States which was not slow in proposing a con nendal snow paul see to help sustain the Cold War.

Many Canajans felt that it was morally wrong to use a strategic material like snow for aggressive purposes and demonstraders quickly appeared outside Hugh Ess diplomatic offices in many cities. Others opposed the Ardic becoming a branch plant of the Mare Can snow industry and more demonstraders paraded on Parl Meant Hill at Oddawa in sub-zero weather. In addition letters were written to newspaper editors, and the Seabee See did a half-hour television show on trapping Ardic foxes.

Always responsive to public opinion, the guver meant tried to dispose of their stockpiles of snow in Yourp, but this was blocked by anti-dumping measures imposed by the E.E.C.

Some effort was then made to expand the domestic market under the Regional Disparity Program, but this would have involved a costly structure of price supports which failed to gain opposition approval in the Housa Comms, the guver meant as usual being in a minority position.

The whole scheme finally came to grief at the next Fed Rull Per Vinshull Conference when Kwee Beck announced that snow came under per vinshull jurisdiction by reason of the property and civil rights sub-section of the Beanay Act, q.v. The conference broke up when Kwee Beck's spokesman stated that they would never permit the wholesale importation of low-cost Ardic snow into the province thereby reducing the number of snow jobs normally available as part of their winter works program.

With this the fragile economy of the Ardic collapsed. There were fewer igloo starts that year than in any previous twelve-month period and Unemployment Insurance was extended to all Esk Moze whether they were looking for work or not, thereby putting them on an equal footing with the rest of the country.

ARM SEE | Royal Military College at Kingston, Untario.

18

ARSEY EM PEE | A para-military police body combining the most distinctive features of the army (red coats), the civil service (red tape), the secret service (Red hunting) and politics (red herrings). Also known as 'The Moundies'.

ASBESTOS	To the extent of your ability. As in: 'You'll haveta make do asbestos you can.'
ASSESSIBLE	Able to be reached. As in: 'The town of Shawvl, *q.v.*, is easily assessible by road from Oddawa.' The nominal form, assessibility, is less common.
ASSESSORIES	Things that go with other things. As in: 'Howja like mnoo dress, Linda?' 'Grade, Susan, an scott matchin assessories too.'

B

BAL OIL — A street in east-central Tronna. Pronounce to rhyme with 'shall boil'.

BAWLCONY — Verandah with access from upper storey of dwelling house or apartment building; gallery in a theatre.

BEANAY ACT — Briddish statute of 1867 providing for the union of Untario, Kwee Beck, Nove Skoshuh and Noob Runzwig. The other provinces came in later at special rates. *See* Sir John, Eh?.

BEARUS — To disconcert. As in: 'Twuz reely bearussing ta seer there.'

BECUZ — For the reason that; since.

BEDDER — The comparative of good.

BEESEE — The most westerly Canajan province.

21

BEIG	A container made of paper, cloth, etc., with opening at top. Rhymes with German *Feig*. Oddawa Valley Canajan.
BEINCK	A building where Canajans keep their money. The traveller who pauses at a crossroads in the Oddawa Valley and sees on the four corners a beer-hall, a Catholic church, a grocery store and a beinck, knows that he has at last reached a town in the Canajan heartland.
BELIAL, STRAIT OF	An arm of the Atlantic Ocean lying between the coasts of Labberdor and Noophun Lund. Forms the northern outlet of the Gulfa Sen Lornz.
BERREX	Buildings where soldiers are lodged.
BERRIE	Town in Untario about fifty miles north of Tronna.
BERRIL	A cylindrical vessel made of hooped wooden staves.
BIDDER	Not sweet.
BLEEDING	Crying like a calf.
BLEWER	A mid-town thoroughfare in Tronna.

BLING YULE | Adjective applied to a French Canajan who has been obliged to learn English to make a living.

BODAYDO | A plant with farinaceous tubers used as food.

BODDUM | The lowest part; the backside. Used as a toast: 'Boddum Zup!'

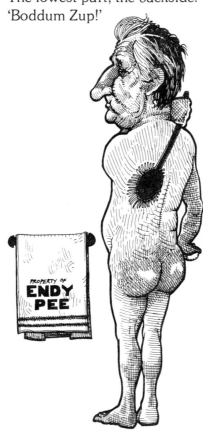

PROPERTY OF
ENDY PEE

BRIDDISH | Of or pertaining to Grade Bridden. Sometimes contracted to Brish, as in: Brish Commwealth.

BRIDDI SHYLES | England, Scotland, Wales and Northern Ireland. Commonly called the You Kay.

BRISH CLUMBYA | *See Beesee.*

BROODLE | Savage, cruel. As in: 'I tellya, Rick, the Leafs' lass game was sumpm broodle.'

BUDDER	Yellow, fatty substance produced by churning cream. As in: 'Id tace bedder with budder.' May be used figuratively. As in: 'Doan budder me yup.'
BUGGETT	A wood or metal pail for carrying water. *See* Torrance.
BUSTA	A transportation term. As in: 'Wenza busta Swiff Kernt?' 'Quorda too.' 'Thang slot.'
BYNOW	*See* Harya.

C

CABBIDAL

The siddy where the seat of plitti cull power is locaded. As in: 'Kwee Beck Siddy is the per vinshull cabbidal.' Also refers to accumulated wealth. As in: Cabbidal gains tacks.

CAB NET

The executive committee of Minsters which, under the Prime Inster, directs state paul see. *See* Paul Ticks.

CANA DUT

A person running for public office who tries to bribe you with your own money to vote for him. As in: 'Heeza cana dut in the necks mewni sippul (fed rull, per vinshull, etc.) lexshun.'

CANAJAN

Four meanings are commonly distinguished.
1. Of Canada or its inhabitants.
2. A person of Canajan birth or nationality.
3. An Anglo, *q.v.*
4. The nash null language of Anglos.

CANAJAN LEEJUN

A vedderans' organization dedicated to re-fighting past wars.

CANDA | The attributive form of Canada, the nation-state of all Canajans. As in: Canda Countsil; Stastistics Canda; Canda Dry, etc.

CENT | The appointive branch of parl meant. *See* Paul Ticks.

CENTRES | Members of the Cent, *q.v.*

CHEWSDY	The day after Mundy. *See* Sundy.
CHOOB	Hollow cylinder; also component part of a radio or TV set. *See* Toob.
CLIMB IT	Canada has three kinds of weather – hot, cold and wet. Hence the only permitted conversational gambits relating to climb it are: 'Hottanuff furya?', 'Coldanuff furya?' and 'Wetanuff furya?' These may be abbreviated to: 'Hot, eh?', 'Cold, eh?' and 'Wet, eh?'. It would be meaningless and also unidiomatic to ask anyone: 'Nice anuff furya?' No such expression exists in Canajan.
COLUMN	Quiet or tranquil. *See* Kam.
COMMA NIZZUM	System of social organization, particularly as developed by Marks and Lennon. The opposite of Free Dumb, *q.v.*
CON NENDEL	Anything for the benefit of the Mare Cans. As in: 'Washington calls for a Con Nendel Wadder Paul See.'
COUNTSIL	Administrative body of municipality. As in: Siddy Countsil, etc.

CUNSERVE TUVS | A plitti cull pardy. *See* Paul Ticks.

31

D

DEE FENCE OF | Carried on for the purpose of resisting attack. As in: 'Winpaig played a dee fence of game throut the firce quarder.' The opposite term is off fence of, as in: 'But Kail Gree played a grade off fence of game.'

DEETROYIT | Rhymes with 'destroy it'. Large Mare Can siddy lying across the Deetroyit River from Windsor, Untario. Other Mare Can places known to Canajans are Buff Low, Tcha Coggo, and Ore Gone.

DETERIATE | To grow worse, to be reduced in quality or ability. As in: 'Stoo bad howeez deteriated (or deteriaded) ladely.'

DIE JEST OF TRACK | The place inside people, animals, etc., where things turn into other things.

DIRDY | In an unclean state or condition; bad (of weather); obscene.

DISBURSE | To break up or scatter. As in: 'The demonstraders were soon disbursed.'

DIZGOVER

To find. As in: 'Car Chay dizgovered the Gulfa Sen Lornz in 1534.'

DODDER

A female child.

DOOAL

Double, forming a pair. As in: Dooal wheels, dooal highway. Not to be confused with jewel, a combat between two persons.

DUT CHELLUM DOES EASE

A disease of elm trees transmitted by bark beetles.

E

EEJA	To bite fiercely, to consume. Usually with adverbial suffix 'lyve'. As in: 'Cmin quick, Susan, ur the mazkiddas, *q.v.*, ull eeja lyve!'
EGG SELLENT	Very good, of considerable merit.
EGG SEPSHUNALL	Onusual, very egg sellent.
EGGS ISLE	Long banishment from one's country.

EGG SPURT	Someone with special skill or knowledge.
EGG ZACK	Precise or accurate. As in: 'I sawer in the egg zack same place as lass time.' The adverbial form is *egg zackly*.
EH?	Rhymes with hay. The great Canajan monosyllable and shibboleth, 'eh?', is all things to all men. Other nations may boast their interjections and interrogative expletives – such as the Mare Can 'huh?', the Briddish 'what?', the French *'hein?'* – but none of them can claim the range and scope of meaning that are encompassed by the simple Canajan 'eh?'. Interrogation, assertion, surprise, bewilderment, disbelief, contempt – these are only the beginning of 'eh?' and already we have passed beyond the limitations of 'huh?', 'what?', *'hein?'* and their pallid analogues.

To begin with, 'eh?' is an indicator, sure and infallible, that one is in the presence of an authentic Canajan speaker. Although 'eh?' may be met with in Briddish and Mare Can litter choor, no one else in the world 'eh?s' his way through life as a Canajan does, nor half so comfortably. By contrast, 'huh?' is a grunt; 'what?' foppish and affected; and *'hein?'* nasal and querulous. Whereas 'eh?' takes you instantly into the speaker's confidence. Only 'eh?' is frank and open, easy and unaffected, friendly and even intimate.

Viewed syntactically, 'eh?' may appear solo or as part of a set of words, in which case it may occupy either terminal, medial or initial position. We shall consider these briefly.

Its commonest solo use is as a simple interrogative calling for the repetition of something either not heard because inaudible or, if heard, then not clearly understood. In this context 'eh?' equals 'What did you say?', 'How's that?' Or in Canajan, 'Wadja say?', 'Howzat?'

According to intonation, the meaning of solo 'eh?' may vary all the way from inquiry (as we have seen) through doubt to incredulity. Here are a few examples:

'I'm giving up smoking.' 'Eh?' (A cross between what? and oh yeah?)

'Could you loan me two bucks?' 'Eh?' (Are you kidding?)

'Here's the two bucks I owe you.' 'Eh?' (I don't believe it!)

'Eh?' in terminal position offers a running commentary on the speaker's narrative, not unlike vocal footnotes:

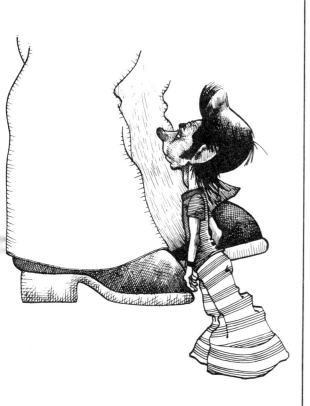

'I'm walking down the street, eh?' (Like this, see?)

'I'd hadda few beers en I was feeling priddy good, eh?' (You know how it is.)

'When all of a sudden I saw this big guy, eh?' (Ya see.)

'He musta weighed all of 220 pounds, eh?' (Believe me.)

'I could see him from a long ways off en he was a real big guy, eh?' (I'm not fooling.)

'I'm minding my own business, eh?' (You can bet I was.)

'But this guy was taking up the whole sidewalk, eh?' (Like I mean he really was.)

'So when he came up to me I jess stepped inta the gudder, eh?' (I'm not crazy, ya know.)

'En he went on by, eh?' (Just like that.)

'I gave up, eh?' (What else could I do?)

'Whattud *you* a done, eh?' (I'd like to know since you're so smart.)

'Eh?' in medial position is less common and so more prized by collectors:

'We're driving to Miami, eh?, for our holidays.' (Like where else?)

'There aren't many people, eh?, that can find their way around Oddawa like he can.' (You know as well as I do.)

'Eh?' rarely appears in initial position. Thus, while one might ask: *'N'est-ce pas qu'il a de la chance?'*, Canajans could only say: 'He's lucky, eh?'

Forners are warned to observe extreme caution with 'eh?' since nothing will give them away more quickly than its indiscriminate use. Like the pronunciation of Skatchwan (only much more so), it is a badge of Canajanism which requires half a lifetime to learn to use with the proper panache.

A teacher at Arm See suggested recently that 'eh?' is not Canajan since it may also be found in the Knighted States, the You Kay and Sow Thafrica. In the same way sign tists have tried to prove that hockey was not invented in Canada, but Canajans remain unconvinced, eh?

ELSIE B.O. | A collateral descendant of Dora, the scourge of Britain during World War I, Elsie runs the Liquor Control Board of Untario in such a way as to make drinking within that province as difficult and unpleasant as possible. As a result, she is held in high disfavour by all serious drinkers and remembered by them with a curse in their libations. Some of her sisters plying their trade in other provinces are Elsie Beesee in Brish Clumbya and Elsie See 'em in Mantoba. A brother, Elby Ess, does the job in Skatchwan.

EM PEE | A member of the Housa Comms, *q.v.*

EM PEEPEE | A member of the per vinshull legislature.

ENAY CHELL | The Nash Null (i.e. Mare Can) Hockey League, whose teams are basically Canajan players in voluntary servitude to Mare Can clubs. Compare multinational corporations which are basically Canajan industries in voluntary servitude to Mare Can corporations; and international unions which are basically Canajan workers in voluntary servitude to Mare Can unions.

END	The commonest conjunction in Canajan. As in: 'On the Parkway south it's stop end go.' Sometimes reduced still further. As in: 'En then I sedter . . . '
EUCHRE ANIAN	An imm grunt from the You Crane. Many Euchre Anians originally settled on the prayer ease where their descendants now consider themselves to be one of the found-in races, *q.v.*
EVER	An intensive widely employed in Canajan. Quite unrelated to English adverbial usage, the interrogative or inverted form is usual. 'Is it ever hot!' (It sure is hot!) 'Didja hava good time at the drive-in lass night?' 'Did we ever!' (We certainly did!) 'Coodja gofer somepm cold?' 'Could I ever!' (You bet I could!)
EYE DENTY	The condition or character of what a thing or person is. As in the phrase Canajan eye denty, the search for which (next to hockey-watching) constitutes the nash null sport of all native sons.

F

FAIL YOURS

Elsewhere in the text we have recounted the saga of Canajan he rows. At this point frankness compels us to tell of two nash null fail yours, both of whom blew it in the same year. 1837 was a very bad time for rebellions. First Lower Canada rebelled under Looie-Joe Pappy No who was born at Mun Treal like his pappy before him. In Upper Canada the rebel leader was William Lyin Mackenzie, a forner from Dundee, Scotland.

The causes of both rebellions were the same only different. But basically it was a matter of outs against ins, with the ins staying in and the outs ending up farther out.

In Upper Canada the famly was still very compact in those days, and when Mackenzie tried to loosen the ties a bit they threw him and his type into Tronna Bay. After Mac had dried himself off he went right on demanding reform and so was considered unbalanced. When reform failed to arrive Mac started a fight in a tavern but took off after the first shot. The militia chased him all the way to Nagra Falls, *q.v.*, where he thumbed his nose at them from an island in the middle of the river.

Mac moved on to the Knighted States, then as now a favourite refuge for Canajans (*see*

Mare Canzation). There he conspired for a while with some Irishmen, the forerunners of the Feeny Anns (*see* Troop Ate Rot Love-In). Eventually he came back to Canada where he hacked out a living as a writer, then as now the last resort of failed Canajans. It wasn't until very much later when his grandson, William Lyin Mackenzie King, took over Canada that Mac got even.

But while things were looking up in Upper Canada they kept going down all the time in Lower Canada. Long discouraged with the plitti cull situation there, Pappy No believed that the creation of an Upper House in Lower Canada would put the province on an equal footing with Upper Canada. When they pointed out to him that there was no Upper House in Upper Canada but only a Lower House as in Lower Canada, Pappy No resigned in confusion from the Executive Countsil and started his own rebellion of 1837.

At first Mac offered to help Pappy, but the offer was sensibly declined on the theory that two losers don't make a winner and Pappy No was already in enough trouble by himself without Mac's assistance. In fact, he quickly followed Mac's example by heading for the Mare Can border before the real fighting started. After a decent interval all was forgiven and Pappy

came back but things were never the same again. Nobody remembered him, and in old age he founded the Seigniory Club at Montebello on the Oddawa River and died. His revenge on hiss tree was almost as good as Mackenzie's since he too left a grandson, Henri Bourassa, who did much to put modern Kwee Beck in the shape it's in today.

The Troubles of 1837 are always referred to as a rebellion rather than a revolution because the Canajans, while undeniably rebellious, were not revolting like the Mare Cans in 1776.

FAMLY ROOM | Part of home used for leisure or social activities. Also known as Wreck Room.

FEBBOO WARY | The month following Jannery.

FED RULL | Of or relating to the central guver meant of Canada. The opposite to per vinshull.

FEUDAL | Vain or useless. As in: 'Leavim lone, Linda. It's feudal targue withim, I tellya.'

FIDA | Term introducing protasis. As in: 'Fida knew weed be short, Gary, Ida taken the both of them.'

FILLUM | Thin layer of very hard water found on the surface of Canajan lakes, etc., in early winner. As in: 'A fillum avice covered the pond.' A fillum is also the long roll of stuff used to take pick shirs with. As in: 'Yagoddinny colour fillum?'

FINEY | In the end; eventually. As in: 'Well, when we finey god there everyoned gaw nome.'

FIRCE | Ahead of others in time, rank or importance. Rhymes with 'curse'. As in: 'The lass shall be firce.'

FISHLE | Duly authorized. As in: English and French are the fishle languages of Canada. Also, a person employed in a public capacity: 'According to an undenfied fishle . . .'

FORNER | A non-Canajan. The adjective is Forn.

FOUND-IN RACES

In keeping with the binary struck shir of Canajan paul ticks (*see* Nash Null Yewnty) there are two found-in races in Canada although not everyone is in agreement about which two. The Bye-and-Bye Commission proceeded on the assumption that Canada was a partnership between the two found-in races of English and French, although it is beyond dispute that the Esk Moze and Injuns were found-in much earlier. While it is true that there was never a partnership between Esk Moze and Injuns, we have little evidence that the English and French were ever any better off. The claims of other groups to the title of found-in races are examined elsewhere (*see* Euchre Anians *and* Loy Lists).

FRAY TRATES | Consonant with the binary nature of Canajan plitti cull life which has been noted elsewhere (*see* Nash Null Yewnty), the guver meant helped unite the various regions of Canada by encouraging construction of a network of transcontinental railway lines. At the same time it kept them apart by a complicated system of fray trates which no one understands. This ensured a state of maximum confusion and dissension while preserving a minimum of efficiency and economy.

As one example of the problems involved, by an agreement reached in 1897 all grain shipments from the prayer ease, *q.v.*, were required, whatever their destination, to move westward through the Croze Nest Pass at very low fray trates. It was soon realized, however, that this would cause much hardship to the Merritimes, *q.v.*, since grain consigned there would have to be trans-shipped by boat from Vancouver to Halifax via the Panama Canal. Opposition critics were quick to point out that the Panama Canal had not yet been dug, which rendered the whole operation not merely uneconomical but almost impossible.

To resolve this impasse recourse was had to a legal fiction. For many years thereafter operators only pretended to ship eastbound grain to the west coast. It was instead sent at the lower Croze Nest Pass fray trates through Four Twilliam (now the Lay Ked) during the night, thereby bringing the railroads to the verge of bankrupture or financial hernia.

Only the discovery that wheat was more important than people saved the day, although the Grand Trunk Railway had already packed it in by then. Fray trates were boosted, while passenger traffic was cleverly discouraged by exchanging freight and passenger cars wherever possible. In no time the railroads were rolling again and the passengers were flying.

FREE DUMB	Our way of doing things. *See* Comma Nizzum.
FRINTSTANTS	For example.
FUCHSIAD	On the condition or supposition that. As in: 'Fuchsiad seer asterta phone me.'
FURN CHUR	Movable articles in a room, such as tables, chairs, etc.
FYE ERR	A conflagration. As in: 'There wuz a three-larm fye err on Bal Oil Street lass night.'

G

GERM KNEE	Your Peen country.
GLADDA SEEYA	*See* Harya.
GODDA	*See* Hadda.
GODDEN	Perfect participle of 'to get.' As in: 'It's godden very you mid in here allva sun.'
GRADE	A number of meanings may be distinguished. Famous, as in: 'Jock Car Chay was a grade explorer.' Very good, first rate, as in: 'I feel grade.' Very well, as in: 'Things are goin grade.' There is also an ironical sense, as in: 'I think it's startina rain.' 'Oh grade!'
GRADE BRIDDEN	England, Scotland and Wales. *See* Briddi Shyles.
GRADE EEL	Very much, considerably. As in: 'She feels a grade eel bedder thi smorning.'

GRADE LAKES | The name applied to Lakes Spearyer, Urine, Mishgan, Eerie and Untario. Together they form the largest body of polluted fresh water in the world. The Grade Lakes are part of the Undefended Front Ear, *q.v.*, and when they were being divided up between Canada and the Knighted States the Mare Cans got more than their fair share of four of the lakes and all of Lake Mishgan. This was done long before Confed Rayshun when Bridden did Canada's bargaining for her. As usual Bridden ended up by giving the lion's share to the Mare Cans, her older and stronger offspring. This is why she is called the Mother Country.

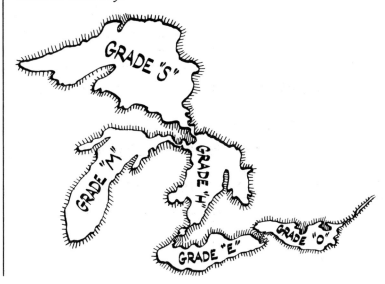

GRADGE	A building for storing or repairing automobiles.
GRAKE UP	Trophy awarded annually for pre-eminence among Canajan professional football teams. The championship game itself, largely conducted by Mare Can players, has been supplanted in importance since the advent of TV by the organized bragging and drinking which accompany it.

GRODGE	*See* Gradge.
GUVER MEANT	*See* Paul Ticks.

H

HADDA

To be obliged to do something. Cognate with Godda. As in: 'I jiss hadda tellum, Susan, I jiss hadda.' 'Well, thass life, Linda, if ya godda ya godda.'

HAIRY

Man's name. As in: 'I'm jiss wilda bout Hairy.'

HAN CHA

Interrogative phrase used to ascertain the availability of something. As in: 'Han cha gottiny matches, Rick?'

HAPPIS

See Quorpus.

HARYA

Like most aspects of Canajan, the salutations upon meeting or parting are highly formalized and call for precise observance.

Set orders of salutation are, of course, established in every language from French to Tagalog by inveterate custom, and may not be altered or departed from without risk of the speaker's being thought an ignorant boor or, what is worse, a forner. Thus, when he is introduced to someone it is mandatory for a Frenchman of the better class to say: *'Enchanté de faire votre connaissance'* and, upon parting, *'Enchanté d'avoir fait votre connaissance'*.

These forms are prescribed by the venerable Académie Française and the trick of dominating the encounter (or departure) is to get in first with the phrase, thereby leaving your vis-à-vis nothing more impressive to say than a rather lame *'Enchanté, Monsieur'* (or *'Madame'*, as the case may be).

A comparable punctilio attaches to Canajan salutational usage. The invariable salutation upon meeting is 'Harya t'day?' whether the object of the remark is an old friend or someone you have just been introduced to for the first time.

Although the phrase clearly contains an enquiry as to the health of the person addressed, authorities are divided about whether the response should disclose the requested or, indeed, any information. If in doubt, the periphrastic phrase 'Priddy good', *q.v.*, may safely be employed or, if more warmth is indicated, 'Fine thankya' is a not unidiomatic reply. But it is perfectly correct to confine oneself to a repetition of the original greeting.

If the opening remark be considered as a gambit, the collocutor may accept by replying 'Howya bin?' thereby restoring the balance of conversational power. If the gambit is to be declined, the relatively neutral phrase 'Gladda seeya' will permit the parties to proceed to the next or substantive phase of the encounter.

Because of limitations of space any discussion of the middle game is here omitted, but some aspects will be dealt with at other places in the text.

Parting rituals are similarly stylized. Among old friends 'Slong' is quite appropriate, although perhaps less satisfactory at the end of a first meeting. In the latter situation 'Seeya gen' (the 'g' is hard) is a little more cordial than 'Nice senior' which does not explicitly look forward to a renewal of the acquaintanceship.

The closing salutation 'Bynow' is telephonese and to be avoided in conversation.

HERALD | Man's name. As in: 'Nowfwee had summon here like Herald Wiltson . . . '

HINGON | To hold the (telephone) line. Rhymes with 'Sing on'. As in: 'Sorry but heez tye dup. Woodja like ta hingon fur a mint?'

HIRE EYES	Multi-storied apartment or office building.
HISS TREE	Study of past events.
HORBLE	Extremely unpleasant, as weather, a noise, etc.
HOUSA COMMS	The elective branch of parl meant. *See* Paul Ticks.
HOWYA BIN	*See* Harya.
HUGH ESS	The Mare Can nation. *See* Knighted States. So convenient has the Hugh Ess been to the development of the Canajan ethos that if the Hugh Ess did not exist it would be necessary to invent it. By the same token, if the Hugh Ess did not exist neither would Canada, much as in physics anti-matter requires matter to sustain it. For this reason, Canada's finest hours have always been dee fence of, witness The Whore of 1812, Confed Rayshun, etc. These and related topics are discussed elsewhere in the text. It may here be noted that the best, perhaps the only generally accepted definition of Canajan is *Not Mare Can.*

HURCHA	Inflict harm or pain. As in: 'Jee, Gary, diddie hurcha?' Do not confuse with Hurja, *q.v.*
HURDLE	To move with great speed. As in: 'Come to the See Enee, *q.v.*, and watch the Sky Divers hurdle through the yair.'
HURJA	To perceive aurally. As in: 'Awrite, awrite, I hurja the firce time!'

I

IDA | *See* Fida.

IDDLY | Your Peen country. Rhymes with 'tiddly'. Along with Bridden, Germ Knee, etc., the source of many post-war imm grunts.

IMM GRUNT | One who comes into the country as a seddler. The name is believed by some to derive from the fact that for years all heavy or unattractive work was reserved for imm grunts. Many people objected to their admission on the ground that they took jobs away from Canajans. When it was pointed out that imm grunts mostly did work which Canajans were unwilling to do, this restriction was quietly relaxed and imm grunts began to do other kinds of work as well. The name has, however, remained.

INN TREST	Concern or curiosity. As in: 'He showed no inn trest a tall.'
INNY	Some, any. As in: 'The lass busses gone, Gary. Izzer inny chansova lift?'
INTA RESTING	Arousing curiosity or attention.

J

JA Second person pronoun, singular or plural. As in: didja, woodja, coodja, hadja, wyja. Often occurs in elliptical phrasal usage: 'Wineja cmover tnite, Linda?' 'Wearja go Chewsdy?' 'Hooja (properly *hoomja*) asta go?' When 'ja' follows after certain consonants (for example 'r') the variant form 'ya' may be substituted. As in: 'Hoorya goint the dance with?'

JAMEENYA Interrogative, usually expressive of surprise or mild disbelief. As in: 'Jameenya reely sawm wither?'

JEWEL *See* Dooal.

JOGGA FEE Study of the earth's features, population, climb it, etc.

K

KABIT, JOHN

Canajans have never been able to make up their minds how to pronounce the name of the man who discovered Canada, or even what part of Canada he discovered. There are some who prefer the New England Kabit, as in 'habit' or 'rabbit'; others call him Kabow, to rhyme with 'Joe Blow'; or Kabott to rhyme with 'why not'.

Whatever his name, Kabit (or Kabow or Kabott) came originally from Iddly by way of Bridden, which was not Grade in those days. He was thus a double forner and well qualified to become a Canajan nash null he row. He was not, of course, the first imm grunt since he made a round trip. The title of first seddler is usually reserved for Looie Hey Bear, also a forner (French) who built a farm at Sault-au-Matelot, so called because he jumped ship there in 1623.

Kabit's discovery of Canada was nothing less than sheer genius (as he told his wife) or possibly blind luck (as it appears to us). While almost everyone else in the fifteenth century who wanted to get to the East was doing the obvious thing and sailing eastward, Kabit for some reason decided to go west. By so doing he tripped over Canada which was in the way.

No one is sure where Kabit landed, but wherever it was he took possession in the name of the King of England who later gave him ten pounds for his trouble. Since Canada has an area of roughly 3,500,000 square miles (not counting water), this was a much better buy than Manhattan Island for which the Dutch rather foolishly paid twenty-five dollars some 129 years later. In fairness it should be said that real estate values had been going up in the meantime because of inflation, but the fact remains that, as usual, the Briddish made the better deal.

The exact location of Kabit's landfall is still a matter of much dispute among sign tists and jogga firs. All are agreed that he landed on the coast of Noophun Lund, except for some who think that it was Cape Breddon, or maybe even Labberdor.

Where he landed is, however, less important for us than the fact that he did so at all since it enabled the Briddish, for a ten-pound payment, to get ahead of everybody else as *the* original found-in race. The French, for example, weren't found-in until 1534 (by Jock Car Chay). We now know, of course, that the Injuns and Esk Moze had been found-in much earlier, but Kabit didn't see them when he landed so they couldn't prove that they were there ahead of him. Also,

since they had not paid any money, as the
Briddish were always careful to do, they were
considered squatters and could be safely
disregarded.

KAIL GREE	The principal siddy of suthren Albirda.
KAM	Serene, quiet or tranquil. The verbal form is common. As in: 'Kam down, now!'
KENTCHA	*See* Kenya.
KENYA	Are you able to? As in: 'Kenya stop whatcher doon en gimmier hand?' The negative form is Kentcha.
KERRY	To convey or transport. As in: 'Kerry me back to Old Moosejaw.'
KETCH	To intercept the motion of. As in: 'Henderson at cenner ice ketches the shot en . . .'
KEWPIE PEE	The Kwee Beck per vinshull pleece.
KIDDY	A young cat. As in: 'Whatza madder, Rick?' 'I can't find the kiddy-lidder, Susan. Whereja puddit?'

KNIGHTED STATES	The Mare Can nation. *See* Hugh Ess.
KWEE BECK	A Canajan province and siddy. Stress falls on the second word. Rarely, Kuh Beck. Just as the simplest definition of Canajan is *Not Mare Can*, so the most convenient way to define Kwee Beck is *Not Anglo (Le Québec n'est pas une province comme les autres)*. Such is the power of the Canajan negative.
KWEE BECKER	A French-speaking inhabitant of Kwee Beck. For English-speaking Kwee Beckers *see* Anglo.

L

LANDIG PROVINCES	The Merritimes, *q.v.*, plus Noophun Lund.
LASS	*See* Firce.
LECK SHIR	An admonition or reproof. As in: 'Mom sure gameya leck shir fur doonit.'
LEER ICKS	The words of a song.
LENTH	The linear measurement of something; the distance it extends. The verbal form is lenthen. As in: 'Sgrade, Linda, butchull hafta lenthen the sleeves.'
LIB RULLS	A plitti cull pardy. *See* Paul Ticks.
LIMINADE	Get rid of; dispense with. As in: 'Shaw peer en liminade the middulman.'
LITTER CHOOR	Books and writings, either of a general or specific place or period. As in: 'Our classes taken Canajan litter choor necks term.'
LORA C. CORD	Like most Canajan pay trots and/or nash null he rows, Lora C. Cord was a forner, an attribute which she shared with Sir John, Eh? (a

Scotsman), Sham Plane (a Frenchman) and
Genrull Wolf (an Englishman). Of the nash null
he rows who made it big, only Looie Real was
native-born (a May Tea).

For Lora C. Cord was a Mare Can by
birth, which explains much about her celebrated
exploit. Long before our tale unfolds she had

come to Canada with her parents, married a Canajan and established herself on a farm in the Nagra Pninsla, when the War of 1812 broke out.

On that fateful day in June 1813 (this was actually during the War of 1813) Lora's aim was not, as hiss tree books relate, to tell the Canajans at Beaver Dam that the Mare Cans were coming since the Canajans had already received this information from the Injuns. Besides, this is too obviously a reworking of the Paul Revere story to hold water. The truth of the matter is that Lora was a double agent and her real purpose was to let the Mare Cans know that the Canajans knew that the Mare Cans were coming, while encouraging the Canajans to think that the Mare Cans did not know that the Canajans knew that the Mare Cans were coming. This was to prove a crucial point, since if the Canajans had known that the Mare Cans knew that the Canajans knew that the Mare Cans knew that the Canajans knew that the Mare Cans were coming, the Mare Can forces might well have been up Beaver Creek without a dam.

To accomplish her mission Lora first dressed her younger brother Rip in one of her well-known starched bonnets and stationed him in the farmyard to milk the family cow. Then while everyone thought her safely at home, Lora made her way some twenty miles through the Mare Can and Canajan lines, stopping off in both camps to spread her message. So successful was this ruse that the Mare Cans almost didn't make it to Beaver Dam at all, in which event the battle of Beaver Dam would never have taken place. It is difficult to say whether this would have affected the outcome of the War of 1812 since to this day no one is sure what the outcome actually was.

In any case, that day's work ensured Lora C. Cord a place in the hearts of her fellow countrymen forever. As for the Mare Cans, we do not know in what way they rewarded this early CIA agent, but significantly a new wing was added to the family home at Queenston in 1814 while not long afterward three new cows and a bull were seen grazing in the back pasture. Local gossips made much of this at the time since Mr. Cord was still away in uniform, but although Lora survived until 1868 she never would tell.

LOY LISTS

Back in 1776 some Mare Can colonists made the mistake of betting on George III instead of George Washington. For backing a loser they were chased out, many of them to Canada, where they and their descendants continued the same tradition.

After the Revolution Lord Dorchester drew up a list (whence the name) of persons who had adhered to the Brish Crown (in the Hugh Ess they were called Disloy Lists because of their Un Mare Can activities). Those of them who could afford it, paid their own way back to Grade Bridden. Those who could not were sent to Canada because it was cheaper to settle them there than ship them all the way back across the ocean.

Once in Canada the Loy Lists received substantial grants of land, thus providing one of the earliest examples of forn ownership, a theme which runs throut Canajan hiss tree.

In many places, (*e.g.* Noob Runzwig and Untario) the Loy Lists became the first English-speaking seddlers, thereby fostering the notion that the Mare Cans were one of the found-in races, *q.v.* People still believe this in some parts of the country.

The Loy Lists or their descendants were probably responsible for what used to be one of the commonest Canajan questions (although it is seldom heard today): 'Where did your father come from?'

M

MACHOOR | Adult, fully developed. As in: 'If you're twendy-one a rover you may be accepted as a machoor stoodent.'

MANTOBA | Canajan province forming the eastern end of the prayer ease. A land of many waters, among them Lake Winpaig which is larger than Lake Untario. It was originally called 'The Postage Stamp Province' because it was collected from the Injuns and May Tea by the Hudson's Bay Company and later traded to Canada over the objections of Looie Real.

MARE CAN Of or pertaining to the Knighted States, its inhabitants or language. *See* Mare Canize.

MARE CANIZE To take over financially or economically; to corrupt or pollute; to impair or destroy the Canajan eye denty by such means. *See* Mare Canzation for the nominal form, Mare Can for the adjectival.

The process of Mare Canizing is not confined to any one area of Canajan life. Besides extending to the classical elements of earth, air and water, it also includes gassa noil, minerals, automobiles, trade unions, undertakers, school books and, what is relevant to our study, language.

The growing Mare Canzation of Canajan has long been the cause of much public concern, particularly in Letters to the Editor. But even the legalization by parl meant of English and French as the fishle languages of Canada has not prevented their Mare Canzation, and the same insidious process has afflicted both Canajan and Joual, the nash null languages. In most parts of the country one no longer hears these ancestral dialects spoken in their pure forms; both are now much corrupted by Mare Can, the language of the invader. One has only to recall the prevalence - indeed the universality - of Mare

Canisms to realize how far the pristine simplicity
and purity of Canajan has been impaired.
'Hopefully'; 'there's no way' (sometimes
abbreviated to 'no way'); 'with it'; 'uptight';
'rip-off'; 'tell it like it is'; and 'ya better believe it'
(partly Canajanized to 'ya bedder believe
it') – these are only a few examples of the growing
deteriation of Canajan. Indeed, it may be only a
matter of time before both Canajan and Joual
capitulate and Mare Can reigns supreme from
sea to sea.

     As a footnote to the Mare Canizing of
Canada one may recall that the process of
winning by losing is a familiar one to students of
hiss tree: witness the economic ascendancy of
Germ Knee over Grade Bridden since 1945. It
seems clear that the Canajans' original mistake
was to beat the Mare Cans in the War of 1812.
As a result the Mare Cans have been on top ever
since. Had the Canajans managed to lose they
would still be receiving forn aid from
Washington to this day.

MARE CANZATION

The familiar term brane drane is used to denote the exodus (much deplored by stay-at-homes and paul tishuns) of talented Canajans – professors, writers, executives, artists, etc. – to the Knighted States. The reverse process (much deplored by stay-at-homes and paul tishuns) is called Mare Canzation.

MAY PULL

A member of the genus *acer*, the arboreal symbol of Canada. In days of yore every Anglo child was familiar with the words of Alexander Muir's grand old song:

> The May Pull lea fa rem blum deer,
> The May Pull lea fa rever. . . .

but for some reason the tune never caught on in Kwee Beck and was gradually phased out in favour of 'Eau Canada'. *See* Nash Null Anthum.

MAZKIDDA	The nash null insect of Canada. A kind of gnat whose bite causes a prolonged itching sensation. Mazkidda-swatting contests are staged every spring at cottage-opening time. *See* Eeja.

MEER	Looking-glass. As in:
	    Meer, Meer ontha wall
	    Hooza fairst wunna vawl?

MELK	Opaque white liquid secreted by female mammals as food, especially for the young. Also used metaphorically, as in the Canajan proverb: 'Snow use cryin over spelt melk.'
MERRITIMES, THE	The eastern Canajan provinces of Nove Skoshuh, Noob Runzwig and Prinz Edwhyland. *See* Landig Provinces.
MERRY	To take a wife or husband; to be united in wedlock. As in: 'Harya, Susan, didja heretha nooz? Rick and Linda are gedding married necks Sadder day!'
MEWNI SIPPUL	Of or relating to a town or siddy. As in: 'Heez spent hafiz life in mewni sippul paul ticks.'
MINTS	Short divisions of time. *See* Quorpus.

MONEY BAG GERENTEE

An undertaking by a vendor to refund purchase price if goods are unsatisfactory. As in: 'Oney Eden's offer zis money bag gerentee.'

MOUNDIES, THE

See Arsey Em Pee.

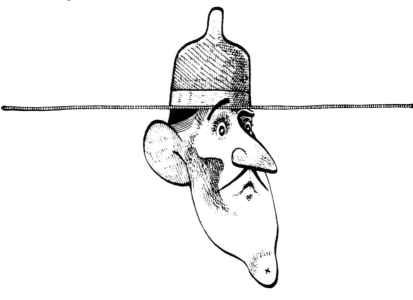

MUNCE

A considerable period of time. Specifically, several of the twelve divisions of the year. As in: 'Jee, harya t'day Linda. Haven't seenya fur munce. Wearya bin?'

MUN TREAL

The largest French Canajan siddy, sidduaded on an island in the Sen Lornz River. Local usage favours the dialectal variant Mon Treal. According to the press, much rivalry is alleged to exist between Mun Treal, the Joual cabbidal of Canada, and Tronna, the Canajan cabbidal of Canada. But of late the two have been growing closer together, at least in appearance, due to the influence of the Knighted States, the cabbidal cabbidal of Canada.

N

NAGRA FALLS

Famous cadaract located on the Nagra Pninsla, a strip of land lying between Lakes Untario and Eerie. Although the Canajans discovered Nagra Falls first, the Mare Cans tried to take them away during the Troubles of 1812. However, the Canajans took them back with the help of Lora C. Cord, *q.v.*, after whom the Canajan or Whore Shoo Falls were named in recognition of her services. Then they gave the smaller ones to the Mare Cans as a consolation prize for losing the war. The Canajan Falls are wider and wetter; however, under the guise of remedial work, done mostly at night with wet-back labour, the Mare Cans are believed to have built up their falls some five feet higher than the Canajan ones.

NASH NULL ANTHUM

Just as Canajans have been much discombobulated in their quest for an eye denty, so they have been more than a little confused in their choice of a Nash Null Anthum. Over a period of time the process of natural selection had pretty well reduced the possibilities to three in all: 'Eau Canada', 'The May Pull Lea Fa Rever', and 'Gossafe Thick Wean', but for a long time theatre audiences were unsure about which one they should stand up for. The short-term

problem was solved by remaining seated for all three of them, but the long-term problem remained.

At this point the guver meant intervened and set up a Parl Meantry Committee to search out and recommend a nash null anthum for Canada. Mindful of the old saying that a giraffe is a horse designed by a committee, the members wisely did not attempt to write a wholly new anthum. Instead, after much deliberation they decided on 'Eau Canada' for a number of compelling reasons:

(1) It had already been written.
(2) A majority of Canajans almost knew the tune.
(3) The leer icks already existed in all four languages: English, French, Canajan and Joual.

Here it should be recalled that 'Eau Canada' is an Anglo version of an old French Canajan boat song. The only verse that anyone remembers is the first, which runs somewhat as follows:*

Eau Canada! How roam a neigh tough land?

*The joual version, which few Anglos know, begins: 'Eau Canada! Tear ruddy nosy you. . . .'

Troop ate rot love-in awl thigh suns come hand.
With glow ingots we seethe here eyes
That rue north Strachan unfree,
Ann's tendon guard, Eau Canada,
Wheeze tendon guard 'fore thee.
(Coarse)
Eau Canada, Gloria's unfree!
Wheeze tendon guard, wheeze tendon guard 'fore thee.
Eau Canada, wheeze tendon guard 'fore thee!

The committee heard much argument to the effect that the use of five tendon guards was redundant and most of them should be cut. Given the nature of partisan paul ticks, much argument ensued between those who wanted to sever all ties and those who felt strongly that the authorized version should remain intact. Still others were of the opinion that it was a bit much to expect 20 million Canajans to learn new words when they scarcely knew the old ones. After prolonged debate a compromise was reached and only two tendon guards were cut, one from the verse and one from the coarse. The last few lines of the verse and coarse were thus revised to read:

Frum faron why d'eau Canada
Wheeze tendon guard 'fore thee.
(*Coarse*)
God key power land Gloria's unfree!
Eau Canada, wheeze tendon guard 'fore
thee.
Eau Canada, wheeze tendon guard 'fore
thee!

The whole thing then went back to the Housa Comms where it was placed in the legislative hopper, never to emerge again. As a result, Canada remains without a fishle nash null anthum and one may in all good conscience remain seated no matter what the band plays.

NASH NULL HE ROWS

Unlike the Knighted States or Grade Bridden, Canada has produced few nash null he rows. This is partly because most potential he rows have gone elsewhere to make it big (*see* Mare Canzation), and partly because of Canajans' innate modesty and reserve. That is why most Canajan he rows have been forners. For a brief survey of successful he rows *see* Troop Ate Rot Love-In. For unsuccessful ones *see* Fail Yours.

NASH NULL YEWNTY

At least as much has been written about nash null yewnty as about nash null *eye denty*. In fact the two concepts are virtually interchangeable. Without yewnty there would probably be no eye denty. And without *eye denty* no yewnty. To make matters even more complicated, it has been suggested that neither nash null yewnty nor nash null eye denty actually exists. If they did, why would one need to write so much about them?

While it is true that around fed rull lexshun time every plitti cull pardy talks of *preserving* nash null yewnty, we have to understand that they are speaking conceptually. Yewnty (like eye denty) has a totemic value which renders it essential to practical paul ticks. Canada could not survive for a single hour without them.

What, then, is nash null yewnty? It may be described in one sentence: Nash null yewnty is what *every* Canajan paul tishun is *for*.

Where paul tishuns differ, however, is about how best to preserve (or achieve) nash null yewnty. This is what fed rull lexshuns are for. Without yewnty there would be no lexshuns. And without lexshuns no talk of yewnty. Such is the binary struck shir of Canajan paul ticks.

The same struck shir dictates that nash null yewnty is made up of many pairs, each part of which simultaneously attracts and repels the other. So we find East versus West; Oddawa versus the provinces; rural versus urban; men versus women; English versus French. For our purposes only the last pair need be considered; the principle in any case is the same for all of them.

It also follows from the binary nature of Canada that two quite different approaches exist to the question of maintaining (or achieving) nash null yewnty. These may be considered briefly as follows.

On the one hand the Sepper Tists believe that Canajans can only really come together in a meaningful way by dividing, and their main plitti cull grouping, the Peek You Pardy, is dedicated to this end. However, the Sepper Tist movement is, appropriately, itself divided into two groups: the Gradualists who see Sepper Tizzum as a slow, evolutionary process (long division), and the Extremists who seek a speedier solution in activism (short division).

On the other hand the Sepper Tists are opposed by the Fed Rullists or Bling Youlists who believe that yewnty can be achieved if enough Anglophones become Francophones. To accomplish this the Fed Rullists have spent millions of dollars on a crash course to make Anglo civil servants bling yule. But so far linguistic baptism by total immersion has produced limited results. Other authorities feel that the only solution lies in intermarriage or a crèche course, but this is clearly a long-term remedy. These two approaches in fact appear to be counterparts of the short division and long division paul sees of the Sepper Tists.

The basic weakness of the fed rull position is that it rests on a shaky premise: namely, that Anglophones speak English and Francophones speak French, both of them languages of civilization. While this may be the case in the rest of the world, it is not so in Canada where English and French are only the fishle (i.e., hypothetical or paper) languages. As we have seen, the nash null (i.e., actual or street) languages are Canajan and Joual, and it is highly problematical whether these, a matter of birth-right, can ever become interchangeable. It is diffi-cult enough to train an Anglophone to be a Francophone; it is almost certainly impossible to train a Canajan speaker to become a Joual speaker. Yet until we can accomplish the latter metamorphosis, any likelihood of a truly bling yule country and hence of nash null yewnty seems remote.

NICE SENIOR | *See* Harya.

NOT BAD | Canajan is unusual among highly-developed languages in that it virtually dispenses with superlatives. Not for Canajans the Mare Can extreme of 'Terrific!' or 'Lousy!' or even the more modest Briddish, 'Awf'lly good' or 'Awf'lly bad'. A Canajan speaker achieves the same effect by an adroit use of meiosis: 'Jalike mnoo soot, Nancy?' 'Not bad.' 'Howdtha Leafs do lass nite, Rick?' 'Not good.'*

One must exercise great care with these and cognate forms, among which Mare Cans and imm grunts may easily lose their way. Thus 'Not bad' really means 'good'; while 'Not too bad' means 'fair', 'so-so' or even 'quite good'. On the other hand, 'Not good' means 'quite bad'. No distinction is made between adjectival and adverbial forms.

A Canajan speaker will rarely if ever say 'bad'. This is not because of any innate desire to avoid wounding the other man's susceptibilities but because 'bad' (and for that matter, 'good') are simply unidiomatic and not available to him

Cf. the fairly recent intrusion of Mare Can 'Great!' Canajanized as Grade! q.v.

under normal circumstances. Thus, if he wishes
to express the sense of 'bad' he must, as we have
seen, resort to periphrasis. And the same rule
applies in adverbial contexts. 'Howza wife feelin,
Gary?' 'Not bad' (i.e., better), or 'Not good' (i.e.,
poorly), or even 'Not too good' (i.e., worse).

NOT GOOD   *See* Not Bad.

NOWER   A division of time equivalent to sigsdy mints.
See Quorpus.

O

ODDAWA	The cabbidal siddy of Canada. Sidduaded at the confluence of the Oddawa, Reedough and Gaddino Rivers.
ODDUM	Between summer and winner, *q.v.*
OFF TEN	Frequently, many times.
OFFUV	Double prepositional construction. As in: 'Rick, woodja kinely takeyer feet offuv the furn chur!'
OH PEEPEE	The Untario per vinshull pleece.
ONCOMFORTABLE	Not comfortable.
ONCOMMITTED	The great Canajan stance.

ONSUCCESSFUL	Not achieving or attaining success.
ONUSUAL	Not usual.
OUIDA	Prefix introducing a conditional construction. As in: 'Two badger cooden come lass week, Susan. Ouida loveda senior.'
OWER	*See* Nower.
OWN SOUND	Town near Jorjan Bay, Untario.

PADDIO Outdoor living area, often paved, adjoining a house.

PAM Inner surface of the hand; also a kind of tropical tree. *See* Pam Sundy.

PAMERSTON The first syllable as in 'Pam'. The town of Palmerston, Untario.

PAM SUNDY The Sundy before Easter.

PARDY 1. A social gathering or reception. As in: 'Hi, Linda! Weir havena pardy Sadder day. Kenya come?' 2. A plitti cull grouping. *See* Paul Ticks.

PARL MEANT The governing body of Canada, composed of the Housa Comms, the Cent, and the Guvner Genrull. *See* Paul Ticks.

PAUL SEE A course of action, particularly in nash null affairs. As in: gassa noil paul see; forn paul see; Mare Can takeover paul see, etc.

PAUL TICKS In Canada, the art of the impossible. The adjectival form is plitti cull. Canajan paul ticks is based on the pardy system, the main plitti cull groupings being: Lib Rull, Cunserve Tuv, Soak

Red, and Endy Pee. A brief discussion of the Canajan plitti cull system is here given because of its linguistic interest.

The Chief Executive was formerly known as the Pry Minster because of a belief which prevailed at the time that the guver meant should be concerned with what went on in people's bedrooms. As a result of this widely-held view, an intensive program of bedroom surveillance was carried out over a period of years by the Arsey Em Pee, *q.v.* After the lapse of much time and several Royal Commissions (including one on the Status of Women) it became apparent that, in fact, very little of interest actually went on in Canajan bedrooms and the whole program was quietly discontinued with a brief announcement that: 'The state has no business in the bedrooms of the nation.' At the same time the Chief Executive's title was changed to Prime Inster, and all-night sittings of Parl Meant were abolished with no discernible loss of efficiency.

The Canajan Parl Meant is bicameral in struck shir, consisting of the Housa Comms or Green Chamber (for go) and the Cent or Red Chamber (for stop). Members of the Housa Comms, known as Em Pees, are elected at quinquennial fed rull lexshuns held every four years. Members of the Cent are called Centres and are appointed for life by the guver meant in power. The Cent was intended to be the place for 'sober second thoughts' about proposed guver meant legislation. For this reason Sir John, Eh?, *q.v.*, although a nash null he row, was never made a Centre.

Plitti cull sign tists equate the Housa Comms and the Cent to a Lower House and an Upper House, although when the parl meant buildings were constructed in 1867 or thereabouts both chambers were sensibly located on the main floor. This was done to avoid any unfavourable comparison based on altitude, and also because elevators had not yet been invented and no one could agree on who should walk up the stairs.

This equitable arrangement, which has continued down to the present day, permits plitti cull debates and name-calling to be conducted simultaneously in both chambers at the same level, thus keeping Em Pees and Centres fully occupied while all important decisions are being made by the Cab Net, *q.v.*

PAUL TISHUN

A practitioner of paul ticks, *q.v.*

PEDAL	Part of the corolla of a flower. As in: 'Hey, lookit the size of the pedals on that buddercup, willya!'
PEEDERBURRA	*Also* Peerburra. Municipality in Central Untario.
PEEK YOU	A plitti cull pardy in Kwee Beck. *See* Nash Null Yewnty.
PENTZEL	A thin cylinder of wood containing a core of graphite, used as a writing instrument.
PERADIZE	Heaven; state of bliss; any new resort area or housing subdivision.

PERAGRAPH	A passage in a document or book separated from what precedes it by indenting the first line.
PERALIZED	Crippled, rendered powerless.
PERRY SOUND	A town on Jorjan Bay, Untario.
PICK SHIR	A painting; a graphic impression. Often used metaphorically, as in: 'Dya wameta drawya a pick shir?'
PIDDY	Sympathy; cause for regret. As in: 'Whadda piddy!'
PINE EAR	A person who first enters or settles a region.

PLENNY	Quite, fully. As in: 'It's plenny gooda nuff fur me.'
PLITTI CULL	*See* Paul Ticks.
PRACKLY	Almost.
PRAYER EASE	The western Canajan provinces of Mantoba, Skatchwan and Albirda.
PRIDDY GOOD	Not really very good. *See* Not Bad.
PRIME INSTER	*See* Paul Ticks.
PROSSNT	Along with Cath Licks, one of the major religious denominations in Canada. In some provinces Prossnt children go to public schools while Cath Lick children are sent to Seppert Schools. This helps preserve the ecology.
PRY MINSTER	*See* Paul Ticks.

Q

QUORPUS Fifteen minutes past the hour. As in: quorpus three; quorpus aid. Other time indicators are: quorda; tempus; happis; tenta. Thus: quorda sevn; tempus five; happis leven; tenta too. The period of sixty minutes is capable of various divisions in Canajan. For example: fie mints; twenny mints; haffa nower; fordy mints. 'Wenl I seeya?' 'Bouta nower.' 'Wendy ryve?' 'Fore thirdy.'

R

RAPE AIRS   Persons responsible for paying mewni sippul property taxes. As in: A delegation of rape airs appeared before Siddy Countsil to oppose hire eyes plans.

RATHER   Rhymes with 'lather' in Canajan.

RAY JOE   Wireless telegraphy.

RECRATION   Pertaining to pastime or entertainment. As in: Recration area.

REEL   Very. As in: 'Mail reel early for Christmas.' Also genuine. As in: 'Izzie fa reel?'

RIDE   Present tense of Rode, *q.v.*

RODE   To have conveyed information, etc., by epistolary means. As in: 'I rode him a lerr boudid, Rick, buddid din dooa bidda good. He never sot.'

ROOT   A territory or round for non-urban postal delivery. As in: Rule Root, abbreviated in writing to R.R. *See* Rowt.

ROWT

A territory or round visited by a person making deliveries. As in: paper rowt, melk rowt, etc. *See* Root.

RULE ROOT

See Root.

S

SCOTT

To have, to possess. As in: 'I tellya, Susan, Walter scott a nerve iffie thinksile wait forum.'

SEE ENEE

The Canajan Nash Null Exa Bishun held annually in Tronna.

SEEYA GEN

See Harya.

SEN LORNZ RIVER

One of the great rivers of the world, stretching from Lake Untario in the west to the Strait of Belial, *q.v.*, in the east. Originally discovered by Jock Car Chay who entered and circled the Gulfa Sen Lornz on his first visit in 1534 but somehow missed the entrance to the river itself. This bothered Jock at the time and he had to come back two years later to find out where all the water was coming from.

SENNER

The middle point; also a group of buildings or stores within a single architectural plan. As in: senner ice; the Teedee Senner in Tronna; Siddy Senner, etc.

SENN ISLE	Showing a decline of the mental faculties in old age; feeble.
SENTS	Sense. As in: 'I tellya, Linda, it jiss dough make sents.' Sents meaning sense should not, however, be confused in Canajan with sense meaning cents. Thus one would say: 'He made me feel like two sense.'
SENZETIVE	Quick to have one's feelings hurt; easily affected by external impressions. As in: 'Sheez too senzetive frone good.'
SEPPERT SCHOOLS	*See* Prossnt.
SEPPER TIZZUM	*See* Nash Null Yewnty.
SHAM PLANE	Samuel de Sham Plane, a forner and the Father of New France, was one of the earliest Canajan nash null he rows. Born in France, he spent many years discovering parts of Canada which hadn't been found yet.
	From the time that he was a young boy Sham Plane had been very good at finding things. He didn't discover Canada, but that was only because it had already been discovered (by Jock Car Chay). But he did discover much of present-day Kwee Beck and Untario, including

the Oddawa River, Jorjan Bay and Lake
Nipissing.

Occasionally Sham Plane lost things as
well. One day while out discovering Jorjan Bay
he slipped and fell on his astrolabe which was
not found again until about 300 years later.

Sham Plane also did much for the Injuns.
Up to that point they had left each other pretty
much alone except for occasional hairdressing
parties. But Sham formed alliances with them
and so taught entire tribes to fight against each
other just like white people. Then he imported
the first missionaries to finish the job of civilizing
them.

Sham was a great colonizer. To teach the
Injuns white man's ways he took their lands from
them and brought in shiploads of people from
France to settle there. He founded Kwee Beck
Siddy and Three Rivers which, as he was unable
to speak English, he called Trois Rivières. He
couldn't count very well either since there is
actually only one river, the St. Maurice. He
encouraged agriculture, cut down trees, invented
pollution and generally put New France on the
map.

As soon as New France amounted to
something the Briddish came in and took it away
from the French, thus demonstrating to the Injuns

the importance of the lesson which Sham Plane had already taught them. This was in 1629 during rehearsals for the Wolf-Mont Kam war games later on. However, the Briddish were too busy sending surplus Scotsmen to the Merri-times, *q.v.*, to bother much with New France so they gave it back to Sham Plane a few years later. Had they not done so it would not have been necessary for Gen Rull Wolf to take it away from the French a second time. It is upon such small points that the great events of hiss tree sometimes turn.

Sham Plane made maps, wrote books, commuted yearly between France and Canada, married a twelve-year-old girl, Hélène Boullé, and died. They named Lake Sham Plane after him. They named Saint Helen's Island near Mun Treal after Mrs. Sham Plane.

SHAWVL A town in Pontiac County, Kwee Beck, lying north-east of Oddawa.

SHEEHAN EYE One of several well-known recipients of confidences. As in: 'I jiss canned tellier, Susan; it's between sheehan eye.' Similarly: 'Between ewan eye.'

SIGN TIST Person well-versed in a branch of signs. As in Plitti cull sign tist; soshul sign tist, etc.

SINS Prepositional or conjunctive aid signifying the passage of time. As in: 'Kail Gree's reely groan sins the lass wore.'

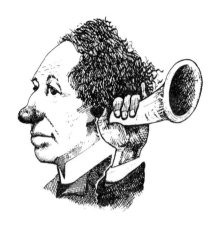

SIR JOHN, EH?

The Father and Mother of his country, Sir John, Eh? started out life with every quality necessary for Canajan greatness.

To begin with he was a forner, always a great boost up the ladder, witness the example of Seedy How (a Mare Can). Since Canajans are taught from their youth onward that they can produce nothing of value, it follows that anything from abroad must be better.

Secondly, he was the very best kind of forner, (*i.e.*, a Scot) - one of that indomitable breed of men who, totally unable to make a living at home, profitably exported bagpipes and banking to the farthest shores of Empire.

Thirdly, he was (so far as Canada is concerned) one of that most fortunate of Scots, namely a Macdonald, a family rivalled in the Canajan Hall of Fame only by the Mackenzies. One need but leaf through the pages of any hiss tree book to realise how much Canajans owe to those doughty Scottish pine ears of another age. And even to this day a boy named Mackenzie Macdonald (or possibly Macdonald Mackenzie) would clearly be destined for great things. That is, if he could ever get people to stop calling him 'Mac'.

John, Eh?'s arrival on the Canajan plitti cull scene came at a critical juncture. In those days the country consisted of Upper Canada and Lower Canada, and the two divisions were engaged in constant bickering and strife. The Upper Canajans felt that because they were upper they should always be on top, while the Lower Canajans objected to being downstream and so always on the receiving end. In an attempt to overcome this rivalry their names were changed to Canada East and Canada West, but the twain never did meet.

The brilliant thought then occurred to John, Eh? that rather than have the Eastern and Western divisions not getting along in a simple union of two, it would be better for them not to get along in a larger union of all the Brish North Mare Can colonies. So taken was he with this idea, which occurred to him one morning while shaving, that he immediately summoned the Fathers of Confed Rayshun to Charltown. There he soon demonstrated to them that a fed rull union would be the solution to all their problems.

Some of the Fathers feared there might be conflict among the future provinces. 'Since none of us is getting along as it is,' he told them, 'we would be much farther ahead not getting along all together.'

Other Fathers said they couldn't afford it, but John, Eh? was not to be deflected from his purpose. 'Since none of us has any money,' he replied, 'let us pool our deficits and print some money. If we keep it in constant circulation among the provinces, the fed rull guver meant will never have to redeem it.'

This display of logic convinced the last doubting Father and the Canajans then petitioned the Brish Guver Meant to pass the Beanay Act which, by dividing everything up among the fed rull guver meant and the provinces, with some overlapping, left things in a state of imbalance that kept everyone on his neighbours' toes forever after.

Macdonald was knighted Sir John, Eh? by the Queen for all his troubles and proclaimed a nash null he row. He was also named Prime Inster of the new nation, a post which he

occupied until the first fed rull lexshun when he
was defeated at the poles. His immediate
successor was named (you guessed it)
Mackenzie.

SKATCHWAN | The middle Canajan province out on the prayer ease; the grainery of the West. Very prehistoric, the parts that aren't cretaceous being quite precambrian.

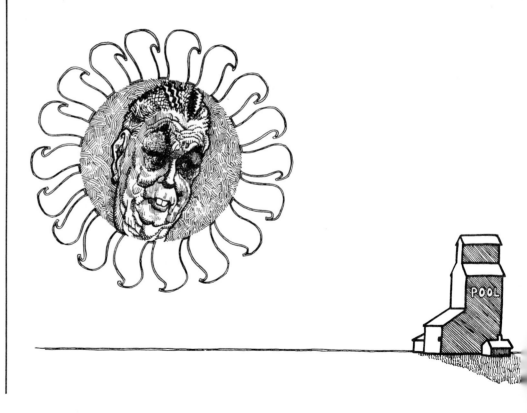

SLONG | The principal Canajan salutation on parting. *See* Harya.

SLOVAT | Motive power of the earth. Witness the Canajan proverb: 'Slovat makes tha world ground.'

SNOTTA | An indicator of resignation. As in: 'Snotta bitta use, Rick. Shwoodent gimmier chance texplane.'

SOAK REDS | Members of a plitti cull pardy. *See* Paul Ticks.

SPEINCK	To slap on the buttocks. Rhymes with beinck, *q.v.* Oddawa Valley Canajan.
SPYDA	Notwithstanding. As in: 'I'm still goan, Susan, spyda whatcha say.'
STRENTH	Vigour; bodily power. The verbal form is strenthen. As in: 'The guver meant's bling yule paul see has (or hasn't) helped strenthen nash null yewnty.'
STRUCK SHIRLEY	Of or pertaining to building. As in: 'The howsiz struck shirley sound.' The nominal form is struck shir.
SUG JEST	To propose. Also occurs in the nominal form sug jest shun.
SUNDY	The first day of the week. Other Canajan days are: Mundy, Chewsdy, Wensdy (Weddens Day on the C.B.C.) Thursdy, Fridy, and Sadder Day (or Sarrday).

SWEDDER | Knitted woolen garment covering upper part of the body.

T

TAMARA

The day after today.

TELECANAJAN

As befits a laconic people Canajans are the world's greatest users of the telephone. This seeming paradox may perhaps be explained by the fact that most Canajan telephone users aren't saying anything, as any innocent eavesdropper can verify. To help conceal this a mini-language has been developed which gets them through the exigencies of disembodied conversation without facial or manual aids.

Canajan telephonese, or telecanajan, bears traces of brachylogy. It is strongly marked by apheresis, litotes and apocope, while dieresis, syneresis and, above all, stichomythia are pronounced. Here is a brief specimen:

'Low.'
'Sooin?'
'Snot home. Hooz peekin?'
'Rick. Thatchoo Linda?'
'Ya. Harya t'day?'
'Priddy good, en you?'
'Grade.'
'Whuzz dooin?'
'Nawmuch. Yagoyna tha game?'

'Ya bet. Godda cuppla graze.'
'Hooz plane?'
'Tronna en Deetroyit.'
'Hooja like, Tronna?'
'Na, eye god Deetroyit by two gowals.'
'Zarrite? Lye haver callya?'
'Ya, wenja spectre?'
'Bouta nower.'
'Asterta callme willya?'
'Sure. Seeya.'
'Bynow.'
'By.'

TEMPA CHOOR	The degree of heat or, particularly in Canada, of cold. As in: 'The present tempa choor outside our stoodios is aid degrees above zero.'
TEMPUS	*See* Quorpus.
TENTA	*See* Quorpus.
THANG SLOT	A verbal expression of gratitude for something given or done by another.
TOB	Opposite of boddum, *q.v.*
TOOB	*See* Choob.

TORE SHIR | The infliction of severe pain. As in: 'Mnoo shoes look good, Susan, bud they're tore shir to wear.'

TORRANCE | Large quantities of water. As in: The rain came down in torrance (alternatively, in buggets).

TRONNA | The cabbidal of Untario and largest Canajan-speaking siddy in the world.

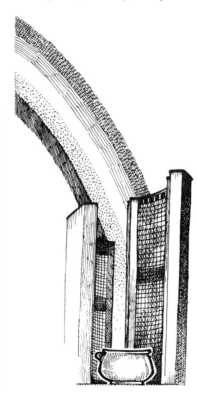

TROOP ATE ROT LOVE-IN The quality which Canada commands in all her sons. Despite this adjuration Canada has produced few troop ate rots and even fewer nash null he rows. One such was Darsima Gee, assassinated at Oddawa in 1868 by members of an early feminist group, the Feeny Anns or Mothers of Confed Rayshun. Others discussed elsewhere in the text were Looie Real, Sham Plane, Sir John, Eh?, Jock Car Chay and Lora C. Cord.

TUDGE To reach; to come in contact with. As in: 'He prackly tudged boddum wennie dove.'

TWENDY Twice ten. One counts thus in Canajan: twendy (or twenny), thirdy, fordy, fifdy, sigsdy, sevendy, eighdy, ninedy (or niney), a hunnerd.

U

UNDEFENDED FRONT EAR

Originally the Canajan-Mare Can boundary line. In view of Canada's inability to Keep the Mare Cans Out, the expression is now largely meaningless and exists on the one hand as a political cliche and on the other as a reference to the invasion of Canada by Hugh Ess television.

W

WADDER LOO   Town adjoining Kitchner, Untario.

WINNER   The principal Canajan season, immediately
preceding summer.

WINPAIG	The cabbidal siddy of Mantoba.
WORSH	To cleanse oneself or one's clothing.
WRENCH	To worsh lightly with wadder.

Y

YAGODDINY

Interrogative to ascertain the availability of something. As in: 'Yagoddiny ornjuz? melk? etc.'

YASKT

To make all necessary enquiries; to request information. As in: 'I'm awfully glad yaskt.'

YESDAY

The day preceding today.

YOMEE

Rhymes with 'show me.' Indicator of pecuniary or other obligation. As in: 'Yomee twenny sense.' Or 'Yagodda tellme, Linda. Yomeea nanser.'

YOU ESS

See Hugh Ess.

YOU KAY | *See* Briddi Shyles.

YOUR PEEN | Of or pertaining to the connent of Yourp. As in: 'Since Grade Bridden joined the Your Peen Comm Marked wherezit leave the Brish Commwealth?'

YUD | Conditional statement expressing will or intention. As in: 'Untario - izzer inny place yud rather be?'

Z

ZARRITE Interrogative response to an affirmative verbal statement, often indicating mild disbelief. As in: 'Susan, Ike ud reely gopher you!' 'Zarrite?'

ZIFF As would be the case if. *See* Preface.

ZMARRA FACK Introductory verbal aid. As in: 'Zmarra fack I wuz jiss goy nowt wenya rived.'